RAVEL

NOVELLO SHORT BIOGRAPHIES

Christopher Palmer

NOVELLO
Borough Green, Sevenoaks, Kent

© Novello & Company Limited 1974

PRINTED IN GREAT BRITAIN BY
NOVELLO AND CO LTD, BOROUGH GREEN, SEVENOAKS, KENT

RAVEL

7 MARCH 1875—28 DECEMBER 1937

By CHRISTOPHER PALMER

Maurice Ravel was born in 1875 at Ciboure, a small fishing-port in the Basses-Pyrénées, between St. Jean-de-Luz and the Spanish frontier. He was of mixed Swiss-Basque descent, Swiss on the side of his paternal grandfather and Basque on his mother's. Curiously, Basque folk-music plays a negligible part in Ravel's work, whereas there is a pronounced *Southern* Spanish element running right through it—the Spain of his dreams.

Almost immediately after Maurice's birth the family moved to Paris, where three years later a second son, Eduard, was born. Joseph Ravel, their father, was a man of wide culture who encouraged his elder son's enthusiastic, though not precocious, musicality. Maurice began taking piano lessons at the age of seven, and in 1889 progressed to the Paris Conservatoire. This was the year of the Great Exhibition, at which there were opportunities to hear not only the exotic musics of Java and Bali but also all-Russian programmes played by the Colonne Orchestra under Rimsky-Korsakov, whose vivid sense of orchestral colour either then or at some later stage, impressed Ravel deeply.

Promoted to Charles de Bériot's piano class, Ravel made the acquaintance of a young Spanish pianist named Ricardo Viñes, who was to become a life-long friend and devoted interpreter of his works. Together they played Chabrier's *Valses Romantiques* for two pianos to the composer, for whom Ravel always expressed warm admiration. Another important encounter of these years was with Erik Satie, later to become the musical mascot of the group known as *Les Six*. Ravel freely acknowledged the influence of both these composers on his own work.

For counterpoint Ravel joined Andre Gédalge's class, and also attended Fauré's composition seminars. He became to maturity very quickly and his first characteristic work, the *Habañera* for piano, was completed in 1895. This is an accomplished little piece epitomising the composer's twin loves of Spain and the dance; it was later orchestrated and included in the *Rapsodie Espagnole* of 1907.

The first performance of the *Habañera* in 1898 was by no means a success, and the *Shéhérazade* overture of 1899 fared even worse. Ravel later withdrew it, but retained some of the material for use in the three songs for orchestral accompaniment bearing the same name. Better known is the *Pavane pour une Infante Défunte,* a little piano piece whose plaintive melancholy, discreetly handled, can be appealing.

In 1901 there appeared *Jeux d'eau,* inaugurating a new epoch in the literature of the piano. Its technical innovations —a development of Lisztian experiments in the higher reaches of the keyboard and the creation of an impressionistic haze through use of the pedal—undoubtedly influenced the piano idiom of Debussy. The writing bristles with difficulties, but the mood for the most part is placid and contemplative.

In the same year Ravel made the first of his four attempts to win the *Prix de Rome* but had to be content with second prize. In 1902 he again competed unsuccessfully, but sought consolation in the completion of a String Quartet admired by Debussy though sharply criticised by Fauré. (This work is now firmly entrenched in the repertoire.) Ravel's third attempt to win the *Prix de Rome,* in 1903, was again doomed to failure; but, nothing daunted, the composer produced the three afore-mentioned *Shéhérezade* songs, which are among the best of his early works. They are settings of three poems by his friend Tristan Klingsor, who, along with Ravel, belonged to an artistic clique known as *Les Apaches.* Both words and music explore a rich vein of self-indulgent nostalgia: swift and kaleidoscopic in No. 1, langorous and seductive in No. 2 (the arabesque-like writing for the flute anticipates the mime scene in Part III of *Daphnis et Chloë*), wistful and reflective in No. 3. The accompaniment is scored for full orchestra and the music has a warmth and vibrancy rare in later Ravel.

For a fourth and last time in 1905 Ravel tried for the *Prix de Rome*, but this time was not even allowed to enter the competition. A scandal ensued, bringing about the resignation of the director of the Paris Conservatoire, Théodore Dubois, in favour of Fauré. Ravel preserved his usual air of ironic detachment throughout the affair; he was enjoying a yachting trip in Holland as the controversy raged. On his return, however, a period of prolific creativity set in. His social life revolved not only around the *Apaches* but also the Godebskis, a Polish family who probably came as close as anybody could come to Ravel. Their soirées attracted many Parisian cultural celebrities, including Cocteau, Gide, Valéry, Milhaud, Auric, Stravinsky and even Diaghilev. Not a year went by without some new masterpiece from Ravel's pen—this was the happy prime of his life. 1905 was the year of the *Sonatine* and *Miroirs*, both for piano. The latter was a suite of five pieces, each dedicated to one of Ravel's fellow *Apaches;* two of them (*Une Barque sur l'Océan* and *Alborado del Gracioso*) were later orchestrated. Also significant were the *Histoires Naturelles*, settings of five prose-poems by Jules Renard, which like so many of Ravel's early works had a *succés de scandale* at their first performance. As in Debussy's *Pelléas et Mélisande* and later in Ravel's own *L'Heure Espagnole*, the vocal line closely follows the inflexions of the speaking voice, whilst the main musical argument is upheld by the piano. At the same time appeared the *Introduction and Allegro* for harp septet—in effect a miniature harp concerto of slender proportions, lightweight in texture and of beguiling beauty.

1907 brought two of Ravel's best-known works, both with strong Spanish affiliations—the orchestral *Rapsodie Espagnole* and the one-act opera *L'Heure Espagnole*. The *Rapsodie* was Ravel's first orchestral work, a riotous feast of colour but little more. One is reminded of Stravinsky in conversation with Robert Craft: 'It is not, generally, a good sign when

6

the first thing we remark about a work is its instrumentation; and the composers we remark it of—Berlioz, Rimsky-Korsakov, Ravel—are not the best composers'.*

L'Heure Espagnole has been aptly described as a miniature pornographic vaudeville, and there was much in Franc-Nohain's spicy libretto to attract Ravel. It opens with an ingenious orchestral prelude depicting the interior of a Toledo watchmaker's shop—clocks striking at different intervals, a mechanical cock crowing, an automaton blowing his trumpet, an artificial bird twittering, marionettes with their hurdy-gurdies. These seem to be, paradoxically, the true *dramatis personae* of the opera, and the supposedly flesh-and-blood characters find themselves reduced to the stature of marionettes. The final vocal quintet in habañera rhythm may well have been suggested by *Don Giovanni*, reminding us of Ravel's description of his own music to his pupil Vaughan Williams as 'tout à fait simple, rien que Mozart . . .'

Two new piano suites of markedly contrasting character occupied Ravel in 1908—*Ma Mère l'oye* and *Gaspard de la Nuit*. *Ma Mère l'oye* represents the quintessential Ravel. He was nowhere more at home than in the fairy-tale world of Perrault, Madame d'Aulnoy, and Leprince de Beaumont; and only in certain parts of his later opera *L'Enfant et les Sortilèges* did he write music of such affecting tenderness as here (particularly the closing bars of *Les entretiens de la belle et de la bête*). There is no more enchanting introduction to Ravel's art. *Gaspard de la Nuit* is on a much larger scale, and arguably the greatest of his piano works; the three Bertrand passages on which the triptych is based prompted the first overt manifestation of a certain macabre streak in the composer's character. The first piece, *Ondine*, is a scintillating evocation of splashing water and illustrates Ravel's ability to think in terms of enormous melodic sentences; the second, *Le Gibet*, broods dolefully around its persistent internal pedal-point; whilst the third, *Scarbo*, is a blood-curdling piece of musical *diablerie* making fiendish demands upon the player's technique.

---

*Conversations with Igor Stravinsky, 1958

A new challenge now presented itself in the form of Diaghilev and the *Ballets Russes* which took Paris by storm in 1909. The services of many of the city's leading musicians were requisitioned. When Stravinsky was putting the finishing touches to *Firebird* and Debussy preparing to consult him about orchestration problems in *Jeux*, Ravel was immersed in what was to prove his finest achievement—the ballet *Daphnis et Chloë*. First produced in the summer of 1912, *Daphnis* as a ballet was not an unqualified success, mainly due to friction and disparity of aim amongst the principal personalities involved. The music has become better known in the form of two orchestral suites prepared by the composer from the complete score. In composing the ballet Ravel declared himself to be '. . . less concerned with archaism than with reproducing faithfully the Greece of my dreams, which is very similar to that imagined and painted by French artists at the end of the eighteenth century'.

A large orchestra is called for, together with a mixed chorus. The individual dances are all of them miracles of characterization, but some of the most memorable music is reserved for the opening of Parts I and III. The first evokes 'Une après-midi claire de printemps' though the swaying fourths of the distant wordless chorus, the second (*Lever du jour*) brings a broad-spanned arch of cello melody into focus beneath rippling woodwind figuration. The concluding *Danse Générale* undoubtedly served as the model for the finale of another great French twentieth century ballet, Albert Roussel's *Bacchus et Ariane* (1931).

The *Valses Nobles et Sentimentales* were a byproduct of the three years Ravel had spent on the score of *Daphnis*. Conceived originally for piano, the work was later orchestrated and in 1912 presented as the ballet *Adélaide ou le langage des fleurs*. Brittle in texture and uncompromisingly astringent in flavour, it is really among the least accessible of Ravel's works, though frequently played and recorded. Its ironic undertones anticipate the great choreographic poem *La Valse* of 1920, but lack its lurking menace.

In 1913 Ravel went to work with Stravinsky at Clarens in Switzerland on a composite reconstruction of Mussorgsky's

Khovantshchina, commissioned by Diaghilev. At the same time he composed his *Trois Poèmes de Stéphane Mallarmé* for voice and an ensemble consisting of piano, string quartet, two flutes and two clarinets. The instrumental technique shows the influence of Schoenberg's *Pierrot Lunaire* of which Stravinsky had had a score by him at Clarens. The *Trois Poèmes* is an enigmatic and profoundly searching work, unique in texture and idiom and laced with a degree of dissonance unusual in Ravel. With the Piano Trio completed just after the outbreak of war, in August 1914, we are back on more familiar ground. An elegiac *passacaille* forms the emotional core of this work, striking a note of tragedy which the finale—resplendent with massive piano chords cleaving through a haze of string trills—tries not altogether success-fully to counteract. Nevertheless, it is one of the most sheerly thrilling pieces Ravel ever wrote.

Ravel had a strong social conscience, and though his small stature and light weight could easily have exempted him from military service, he would not rest until he had enlisted. Eventually he became an ambulance driver at the front, but his health soon broke down under the strain; the added blow of the death of his mother, to whom he had been deeply attached, left him at the beginning of 1917 a physical and emotional wreck, and he was discharged from the army. By the summer of the same year he was so far recovered as to be able to start work on *Le Tombeau de Couperin,* a suite of piano pieces (later orchestrated) conceived as a tribute to the French clavecinists of the 18th century. It represents a flawless reincarnation of the spirit of the *forlane, menuet,* and *rigaudon.*

For the next year or so Ravel lay fallow, but in the winter of 1919 he was engaged upon a tribute of a very different kind—to the Waltz King himself, Johann Strauss. *Wien,* or as it later became known, *La Valse,* is not so much an orch-estral *tour-de-force* as an ironic Mahlerian *Totentanz* of gargantuan proportions. It served Ravel as a catharsis for the accumulated bitterness of the war years, the death of his mother, and that sense of emptiness and futility which beset so many artists at home and abroad in the early twenties.

Diaghilev rightly viewed it more as a caricature of ballet than a ballet in itself, but failed to convince Ravel, who was deeply offended. Relations between the composer of *Daphnis* and the master of the *Ballets Russes* had been deteriorating ever since the presentation of a garbled version of the ballet in London in 1914, and this time the rupture was complete.

In 1920, after his famous refusal of the proffered *Légion d'Honneur* (the *Prix de Rome* incident apparently still rankled sore), Ravel turned his attention to a project which had originally been mooted during the war years—the setting of a *divertissement* by Colette entitled *Ballet pour ma fille*, later to become *L'Enfant et les Sortilèges*. The music draws both on jazz and Tin Pan Alley. Ravel was a frequenter of the fashionable *Boeuf sur le toit*, a favourable haunt of the Parisian intelligentsia of the 20's, where he had the chance to hear all the latest American importations in the form of blues and ragtimes. This period marked the beginning of a fascination with jazz characteristics which persisted to the end of his career. *L'Enfant* was completed in 1924-5. It cleverly exploits a Chaplinesque blend of comedy and pathos, and, (particularly in the closing pages) reveals unequivocally the composer's essential humanity and warmth.

Meanwhile, Ravel had been finding much of his time taken up with travelling from one European capital to another directing performances of his works. He visited London in 1922, meeting Conrad, and again in 1923 and 1924, when his new *Tzigane*, a virtuoso showpiece for violin, was first performed at the Aeolian Hall by Jelly d'Aranyi. Other works dating from the mid and late 20's were the *Sonata for Violin and Cello*, the orchestration of Mussorgsky's *Pictures at an Exhibition*, and the *Chansons Madécasses* (commissioned by the well-known American patroness of music, Mrs. Elizabeth Sprague Coolidge). A second sonata, this time for violin and piano, has a middle movement entitled *Blues*.

At the end of November 1927, Ravel embarked on a four-month concert tour across America and Canada, including visits to New York, Chicago, Los Angeles, New Orleans, and San Francisco. A highlight of this tour was a meeting with George Gershwin, whose *Rhapsody in Blue* Ravel greatly admired and to which he was to pay discreet homage in the first movement of his G Major piano concerto.

On his return from America in April 1928 there awaited for Ravel a commission from the dancer Ida Rubinstein, the result of which was one of the most famous pieces of music ever written—the *Boléro*. Here, as with *La Valse,* it is a mistake to regard the work as a mere exercise in orchestral ingenuity. It is an expression of the same type of studied savagery as had characterized *Le Sacre du Printemps* of Stravinsky some fifteen years before. Technically the two may have little in common, but a strong psychological affinity between them remains; the potency of their appeal has increased rather than diminished with the passing of years.

Ravel was at Oxford in the autumn of 1928 to receive an honorary degree as Doctor of Music, and at much the same time the following year festivities were held in his honour in the Basque country. By early 1930 the composition of two piano concertos had been started. The Concerto in G is, as the composer remarked, in the nature of a *divertissement.* If it is marred by a rather meretricious finale, the first movement is an attractive concoction with a prominent 'blue' flattened third in one of the themes of the second group, no doubt in deference to Gershwin. The slow movement is one of Ravel's most sublimely calm inspirations.

A much better work is the Concerto for the Left Hand, commissioned by the one-armed pianist, Paul Wittgenstein. In one continuous movement, it ranks as one of Ravel's most powerful creations. The opening, with the contrabassoon crawling out of the murky depths of the lower strings, is extraordinarily spine-chilling; and the central section, a terrifying jackbooted nocturnal march, is the logical outcome of the nightmare visions of *La Valse* and the *Boléro*. It has also been seen as a premonition of the terrible malady which was to paralyse the composer creatively for the last five years of his life. A set of three songs, *Don Quichotte à Dulcinée,* was all that was written of a projected score for a film revolving around Cervantes' hero; the last, the sardonic drinking song *le bois à la joie,* is comparable in tone and context to Mahler's *Der Trunkene im Frühling* in *Das Lied von der Erde.* This was Ravel's farewell to music.

Any account of the composer's last years makes distressing reading. His health, never robust, had been seriously undermined by the privations he had suffered during the war years, and signs of neurasthenia, cerebral anaemia and amnesia had all at one time or another become apparent. The approach of the final calamity was no doubt hastened by a car crash in which Ravel was involved late in 1932. From this time on he found increasing difficulty in writing, speaking, and co-ordinating his bodily movements, although his intellect remained unimpaired. A protracted tour across Spain and Morocco with his friend Léon Leyritz the sculptor served as a temporary distraction, but in the long run an operation proved necessary; it was unsuccessful and Ravel died on December 28th 1937, a year which had also claimed Albert Roussel in France and George Gershwin in America.

When Ravel late in life heard a recording of the *Prélude à l'après-midi d'un faune* he turned to a friend with tears in his eyes and said 'It was when I first heard that many years ago that I realised what music is'. Ravel emerged in 1895 a complete master of his craft without, apparently, ever having had to learn anything about it; nevertheless, as the remark quoted above clearly indicates, *L'après-midi d'un faune* was in fact the beginning of all his music, and he later repaid his debt to Debussy when the pianistic innovations of *Jeux d'eau* helped shape the impressionist piano style of the *Estampes* and later works (at the time of *Jeux d'eau* Debussy had writtten nothing of any great moment for the piano except the pianistically rather jejune *Pour le Piano*). Ravel was less inhibited than Debussy in proclaiming his indebtedness to the composers whose harmonic originality he admired—Liszt, Grieg, and especially Chabrier and Satie. More overtly than Debussy he championed the cause of the Russian nationalists —there was a deep underlying affinity between him and Rimsky-Korsakov which consisted not merely in a child-like enjoyment of lavishly exotic orchestral colouration but also in their common conception of art, as, fundamentally, artifice. To Mussorgsky he paid practical tribute in the form of an orchestration of *Pictures at an Exhibition* and, in collaboration with Stravinsky, of *Khovanshchina* (Stravinsky said that he was the only musician who immediately understood *The Rite of Spring*). Balakirev and Borodin he also admired, particularly the latter's Third Symphony and *In the Steppes of Central Asia,* and echoes of the Second String Quartet are readily discernible in the Ravel Quartet. Spain was another centre of mutual musical attraction; Ravel's *Rapsodie Espagnole, L'Heure Espagnole, Alborado del Gracioso* and other works are among the most distinguished examples of French musical Hispanicism. Debussy and Ravel shared many literary loves: Maeterlinck, Mallarmé, Verlaine (three poets whom they both set to music) Baudelaire, Poe, de l'Isle-Adam and Oscar Wilde. All these manifold interests and influences so conditioned the aesthetic and intellectual *ambiance* of the period that any musician who reacted to them as positively as Ravel could scarcely fail to find himself cultivating what was in so many respects, as we have seen, their natural musical counterpart and complement-impressionism.

The originality of Ravel's impressionism lay in the compromise he effected between the studied vagueness and sensuousness of Debussian impressionism on the one hand, and the clean hard contours, pragmatism and logic of classicism on the other. His was a sound and creative response to those Debussian concepts of emancipated harmony and the reconditioning of texture which were to have such profound and far-reaching consequences in the future development of music. This 'studied vagueness and sensuousness' is a decisive factor in the structure and sonority of *Jeux d'eau* with its rippling pentatonic arpeggio figuration and illusory, evocative use of open fourths and fifths, major seconds, ninths, elevenths and thirteenths in the harmony; in *Shéhérezade* warmly nostalgic, exotically coloured, anticipating the type of orchestral impressionism verging on pointillism which was to be brought to such a pitch of virtuosity in *Daphnis et Chloë;* in *Miroirs* with its nervous, kaleidoscopic succession of flitting shapes and movements notably in *Noctuelles* and *Oiseaux tristes* (the bells of '*La Vallée des Cloches*' are also a favourite impressionist preoccupation); in the murky openings of *La*

Valse and the Concerto for the Left Hand; in *Gaspard de la Nuit* and the nocturnal scene in the garden in *L'Enfant et les Sortilèges*: and, most originally, in the *Trois Poèmes de Stéphane Mallarmé*, especially No. 3 with its shadowy interplay of opaquely-dissonant harmonic shapes dissolving effortlessly one into another.

This advanced norm of dissonance, greater than Debussy's, gives Ravel's music an edge of piquancy and nervousness which marks it off from the hedonistic self-indulgence of impressionism in the normally accepted sense of the term. Melodically too his lines are firmer, more muscular, more roundly-sculpted than Debussy's, although they too are modally-orientated. Formally Ravel thinks in smaller units; the nearest he ever came to the expansive, all-embracing sweep of *La Mer* was in *La Valse,* for even *Daphnis* is episodic in structure and the composer was obviously most greatly drawn to the clean, sharp, well-chiselled outlines of the smaller dance-forms—viz the *Habañera*, the *Valses Nobles et Sentimentales* and *Le Tombeau de Couperin.*

Ravel's was a classically-objectified art. Rarely given to emotional outbursts or violent demonstrations of feeling, he kept his most vulnerable of sensibilities jealously guarded. No-one ever caught him in the act of composing (he must always have worked at night) and he was loth to make public property of the sources of his inspiration. What, in fact, were they?

Whereas Debussy always worked directly from nature (in the widest sense), Ravel tended to look to *impersonations* of nature. His scores are peopled with animals, fairy-tale characters, toys and mechanical contrivances of all kinds. In Ravel's eyes, stylized representation and the subtlest forms of pastiche were not imitation art—they *were* art. This is all intricately bound up with his complex psychological make-up. Hypersensitive and introvert, Ravel always shied away from intimate personal relationships and was terrified of committing himself to reality in any shape or form. Instead he created for himself a world of artifice and fantasy where his illusions—and no-one was more aware of how illusory they were—could be cherished unshattered. His villa at Montfort l'Amoury was, and still is, an eggshell paradise unpenetrated by the common prose of things; here Ravel found a natural outlet for his emotions, sublimated into reliance upon the heterogeneous array of bric-a-brac with which he surrounded himself. Ravel's music *is* Ravel—cool, ironic, detached, sartorially elegant, meticulously regulated; in short, a tireless quest after perfection. Yet warmth, humanity, and tenderness are by no means excluded, nor are elements of a rather tougher grain. Glimpses of the man behind the mask are rare, but frequent enough to enable us to guage the full depth and scope of his personality. Darius Milhaud, generally unsympathetic to Ravel, has admitted to being moved to tears by the closing bars of *L'Enfant* ('il est bon, l'enfant, il est sage') and the same special quality of genuinely-felt but distilled emotion informs the dragonfly's aria in the same work ('sais-tu ce que réflétaient mes beaux yeux?') *Les entretiens de la belle et de la bête,* the sublime love-music in *Daphnis,* the slow movement of the G minor concerto. *La Valse,* the Boléro and most of all the Concerto for the Left Hand are by contrast so sombre-hued, dramatic and even scarifying that they almost suggest some kind of Jekyll and Hyde-type schism—this quiet unassuming dapper little man with his bland air of seigneurial correctitude, to what form of psychic disturbance had he fallen prey that he should be assailed by such traumatic visions? We can ever sense Ravel's terrible loneliness, his longing for human contact, his frustration at its being denied him—can we perhaps see in the insidious fascination jazz exerted over him not merely a child-like infatuation with a new toy, but rather an awareness and response to the deep sadness of the blues and the desperation underlying the frenzied rhythmic contortions of fast jazz? If fuller details of Ravel's personal life ever come to be made available, these are questions they may help us to answer.

It has often been contended that Ravel had written himself out by the end of the war, but this is only partly true. His later works show him branching out in a number of new directions: *L'Enfant et les Sortilèges* reveals a flair for comic opera, the *Chansons Madécasses* are unique in their sonority and emotional *ambiance* and in the Concerto for the Left

Hand not only are new areas of sensibility exposed but also certain possibilities inherent in the interpenetration of 'classical' forms by jazz. Ravel himself felt that he was far from being a spent force as a composer. 'J'avais tant de musique encore dans la tête et maintenant c'est fini pour moi' he is reputed to have said on the last occasion on which he was present at a concert of his works, and the signs are that he was not deluding himself. Ravel was not a 'great' composer in the sense that Debussy was 'great'; he blazed no new trails, founded few schools, even spawned few imitators. As a musical personality he was, nevertheless, unique. His craftsmanship was flawless, his sensibilities finely attuned—and for many people he has come to stand as the epitome of the Gallic spirit in music.

List of Ravel's Principal Works

Piano music

Pavane pour une infante défunte	1899†
Jeux d'eau	1901
Sonatina	1905
Miroirs	1905†
Ma Mère l'Oye (duet)	1908†*
Gaspard de la nuit (after Aloysius Bertrand)	1908
Valses nobles et sentimentales	1911†*
Le Tombeau de Couperin	1917†
Concerto for piano and orchestra, G major	1931
Concerto for piano and orchestra (left-hand)	1931

Orchestral music

Rapsodie espagnole	1907
La Valse, choreographic poem	1919-1920
Boléro	1927

Ballet

Daphnis et Chloë	1909-1912

Vocal music

Shéhérazade	1903
Histoires naturelles	1906
Trois Poèmes de Stéphane Mallarmé	1913
Don Quichotte à Dulcinée	1932

Chamber music

Chansons madécasses	1925-1926
String Quartet, F major	1902-1903
Introduction and Allegro	1905-1906
Trio	1914
Sonata for violin and cello	1920-1922
Sonata for violin and piano	1923-1927

Operas

L'Heure espagnole	1907
L'Enfant et les sortilèges	1920-1925

†also orchestrated   *also ballet